Out of the Dark

A collection of poems

by

Brian Crockett

Published by Brian Crockett

ISBN: 978-1-63491-600-4

Covert Art by Amelia Crockett

Printed on acid-free paper.

First Edition

Dedicated to my wife Amy;
Who held my hand through many dark paths
And never let go.

Contents

Preface

It is a truism that authors should only write what they know. The only change I would make to that statement is that, in the end, a writer *can* only write what he knows.

I wrote, edited and re-edited these poems over sixteen years with many breaks in between during which I forgot they existed. It wasn't until I saw the Robert Frost Farm in New Hampshire that I was inspired to start writing again, which struck me as very fitting.

These poems aren't only what I know, but what I *knew* and the difference is essential. There is suffering and loneliness in these poems; they are the work of someone whose only companion for many years was his own thoughts, memories and soul.

These poems are also a journey from aloneness and injury to a place of belonging and healing with a few hopeful moments scattered along the way. In the end there is some illumination to bring everything together. Evidently the light at the end of the tunnel didn't belong to a freight train.

Lastly, these poems are a goodbye to that loneliness and a warm hello to life and hope. If there is darkness and suffering, it is to prompt eager anticipation of light and peace. If there is loneliness and hollowness, it is to awaken a hunger for belonging, acceptance and satisfaction.

There is shadow under this red rock.
Come in to the shadow under this red rock
And I will show you something far greater
Than your shadow at morning striding behind you
Or your shadow at evening rising to meet you,
I will show you fear in a handful of dust.

T.S. Eliot, The Wasteland

Harvest

Fields sown with feelings bloom
With glass blossoms.
They are heavy.
They are pendulums in gentle breezes;
Lodestones in storms.
They fly only in reflection
Reflecting the passing, pregnant sky.
They are poetry in motion,
Moving as the earth moves.
Reflecting color while colorless,
Capturing emptiness and smiling back.
Fields sown with feelings bloom
In harvests of broken glass.

Resentment

Cigarettes in corner cupboards
Hidden behind corncob prongs;
Coiled serpents scaled in cancer
But cancer is a sweet perfume.

Every evening, secret sneaking,
Past windows staring empty gloom;
Catching glimpses in reflections,
Anticipating open wounds.

In the Image

Cradle cages twist and shudder
In winds that rot in sultry fumes.
These winds pour out bitterness
And exhalations from the womb.
Breathing in the sighs and sorrow
Imbued to marrow in fleshly tomb;
Stillborn children dressed in glass,
Each embrace brings scarlet blooms.

Daddy tell your children stories.
Daddy hold your children tight.
Daddy promise you will never
Let your children out of sight.

Exhale all your stagnant sorrows,
Spill them in your blushing bride.
Fog the glass your children dream,
Scratch them with stiletto sighs.

Mommy hold your children tighter,
Crack the glass and break the seed.
Children reflect what their parents
Left unknown in their need.

Cubed Life

Days that end with Y begin
On a sour note, sweet with familiar
Loathing at the loafing
Grey walls that bleed boredom
Beneath band-aid calendars, photos, forgotten
Memos to remember. They stain
Spreadsheets, bed sheets, budget.
They inhale color.
They ooze into doorstop days,
Eating baseball and yard work;
Relentless, meaningless,
Until all days are grey and never end
But always begin
With why.

Funeral

I am cocooned in a ripe grave
Breathing the memory of meaning.
I am suckled in insignificant significance
Dripping from trees that nurture cadavers.

It spells, in the dark, in inverted Braille;
It spells for the dead.
It spells science, reason, emotion,
And all the tools of conniving men.
Their roots cradle my back
Singing in muted refrain:

me.
I feed the roots and trees which feed
Other men,
Until they join the cradled grave.
We sing, in Braille,
The memory of meaning
Even as meaning drains away.

An Introduction to Postmodernism

This is the pride of Japan standing as tall as a cucumber:
It is a river of swords
Dancing around the volcano,
It is the primordial sea and sky
Hung like a war bow,
That Calvin Klein would die for.

This is the height of my finger standing as tall as a
cucumber:
It is the color Gilgamesh paints the aurora borealis,
It is the feel of a monkey's skin
When viewed in a mirror.
This is the fury of tropic love
And deserted islands:
It is cutting a grizzly's claws while it hibernates,
It is dressing the sun in a ballroom dress
And asking her for a smoke.

This is the genie in an iron casket as long as a cucumber:
It is a non-dairy diet of melon, soap and cheese.
It is staying at a five-star hotel and asking for your money
back.

In Remembrance

Fly away bird of prey.
Fly far, far away.

The heavens bleed
Light, eclipsed in winging shadows,
Onto delicate weddings bands
That drink it like wine.

We feed the dark things.
We are the dark things.
Darkness drinks illumination
Until illuminated
And it doesn't seem so dark anymore;
Hiding broken syringes,
And bloody bottles breaking delicate wedding bands.
Sometimes sickles resemble scalpels,
Shadows hold doctors and butchers.

Thirsty sidewalks sop life like
Sponges beneath guttering electric lights.
Precision wounds adorned with wedding bands
That tell stories and morals
On every pulsing line.

Mothers should tell their children never
Talk to strangers.

Fly away sweet bird of prey.
Fly far, far away.

Enemy Mine

Cobwebs sleep in corners
Draping vacant holes in spectral
Recitations of children's philosophy.
Drawn shades stare with blank,
Pallid faces framed in teasing
Strangled sunlight halos.
Stagnant shadows slumber
In tepid depths of lost dreams;
Following pheromone trails
Swarming, nesting upon the forgotten
Carcasses of petrified
Private sin.

Long walks in tight circles
Reveal dust burial shrouds pulled
Over writing awards with broken stands,
Photographs bound by tarnished silver
And yellowed letters kept in the
Original envelopes; praising my
Sensitivity, sense of humor
And bitterly romantic soul
Stashed within a rusted safe.

Even recent troubles pound a path
Into squeaking floor joists
And released against a cracked, scowling wall
In raging fear.

Consciousness breathes a weary calm
While I reread those letters, look over
Those photographs and awards
That I know so well.

When freedom urges me onward
It blinds me in panic of sunlight.
It dances like a marionette to unlock
All the doors, dungeons, cages
And hide beneath the sweet blessing
Of bed sheets, pillows
While this world gums its prey.

Rats' teeth gnawing on walls
Gouge accusations into troubled dreams
While bat songs poetically torture ears
Turned from, but listening to,
The reminders of another world
That will not wait forever.

Music Box

I walk through a forest
Of naked life, bare with a sincere
Splintery lewdness.
Bold, like a spider in
A well-lit room,
While its melody carries on the wind.

Trees arise from the earth
Sheathed in cool,
Packed whiteness.
A bird glares at nature's nakedness
While its melody carries on the wind.

One tree leers through its hole
At the frozen passage,
Into a wintering party of
Withered woods that
Bask along their lakeside resort.
A childlike splash,
A mother catches the sound
Of its melody carried on the wind.

Light Kiss, Dark Kiss

If I could kiss your wrist.
If it is your wrist, but not your wrist, but your fist.
Strengthening your fist, your wrist,
Your ring.
If I could kiss your ring, your ring on your wrist is soft but is not
But should be
But is bliss.
I will kiss your bliss.

I will scourge your fetish; your fear that you love.
The light that you hate,
Light but more light than light,
Darker than dark but not
And lighter than the dark that you love.

The light in a mug, puddles around a stein,
And dark barley pools begging autographs from
Jumping Jack Flash.

The dark under a rock,
Underground and in the sky
But also under the sea,
Above the sea,
Twisted around the sea on my wrist.

And your sea, a flint nickel,
A nickel from low places and mean
Streets that polishes shoes;

Gouges feet, feet that wear shoes and
Hands that don't wear gloves
Or the dark.

Your light is showing, your big toe,
Your eyelash on my foot,
On my ring that is on my wrist that is your wrist
but isn't and is.
The ring in the sand,
My ring from your wrist on a tree, in the sand.
It is sand.
It is my bliss,
The blissful scourge to kiss
This wrist,
That wrist,
And everyone's and no one's.

I demand nothing in the ring be outside
My light dungeon filled with dark steins
Sweating bliss rings on your wrist.
Above and below,
Both and either or
But also and not only but everything that I am.
I am not your wrist.

Torpor Dependency

Caern in a needle
Filthy joy is feeble
Whisper broken bliss
Shadow puppet kiss

Crawl into a cradle
Blissful maggot fable
Pumping prayer vein
Melting molten pain

Cradle in a gutter
Monocidal stutter
Cradle broken murder
Begotten seething whisper

Gutter mortuary
Graceful whispers tarry
Monocidal solace
Forsaking love in silence

Forgiveness

We put prices on ourselves.
A job is 50,000.
A kiss is 25.
Pain is entitlement to collect
Yearly payments of dignity.

Left

Second-hand tattered standards
Wave on droning drones
Ever left.
Polished shoes and rictus grins
Split faces left to right.
March on,
Left two three four.

The transport docks in theological bay
And waiting soldiers storm the beach
From left to right.
The conveyor groans in counter-clock
Filling pine ovaries;
Home to heaven under curfew.
Left two three four.

Circling steps, stumbling feet
Circling Eden's iron tree.
Forsake well-trod paths for
Being well-trod,

And right turns lead ever wrong
Right is wrong.
March left;
Left two three four,
Left two three four.

A Trail in the Woods

One muted sun winks through
Scornful clouds that
Hide their faces from me.
The heavens strain away
As bloodless arms supplicate
In a dead man's trance.
Ten bare fingers bow
To winter's whispering lips.
I count aloud to seven.

One trail half-erased in creep
Thorns, thistles
Overseen by familiar reign of
Three pine stumps muttering eulogy
That make me forget seven.
Footprints mark in secret moments
Where two children trod
From castles to oceans, back again.
The obscurity falls at my knell of seven.

Stone jaws tease, those familiar tones
Voiced in spectral wind,
Six smooth rocks with wan edges
Frame alluring faces stained in sanguine tones.
Stumbling stones with jagged snares
And breathless spirit,
Beckon with serpentine secrets;
Sibilant, sepulchral,
To countless paths that never were.

I close my eyes
And count aloud to seven.

Busy

The hungry laptop screen
Glares awake at me.
A beacon in the night
Where dreams should have
The right to say:
"Forget about today,
And tomorrow is far away."

But that laptop screen
Shrills a silent scream
Of meetings come and gone.
The dreams they arc
Along and bark
"Tomorrow is not far away!"

The screen bleeding blue-white,
Crisp, corporate inner light
Blanches plastic frames;
Memories
Are swayed, bullied
To stay only as memory.

Summer 2002

A child sleeps in the alley
Between a broken box
And a ripped trash bag,
Where the cracked window leers through
Spider veils drifting with every sigh.

Tombstone streetlights gutter granite curses;
Mute stars smile twilight's breath
Over a clammy throat.
A miniature cadaver sobs at the skyline,
Drowned by the rumbling subway.

One hand clutches a mirror.
It bleeds over passing faces
While nuptial lips part,
Sighing every fairytale.

Washed hands raise an iron cross;
A sword leveled at the heart of the world.
Its shadow bleeds over streets
Anointed by angels' tears.

Exhaling a difference for sixty days,
Exhaling all the difference in the world.
A rising twilight for that child
Born up to the Morning Star.

Good Morning

Sometimes I wake up to tears,
The torment of her choking back
So I don't hear.
But love still hears.

Burdens carried twenty years
In hope chests filled with fetid guilt
That leak her fear,
All secret fears.

Guilt is weightless in the day,
Forgotten in the day's demands;
In twilight rains
Guilt has its way.

Guilt and fear refuse to die
Buried in time yet still they stalk;
And in the day will slink away
But in the dark still work their art.

Sometimes I wake up to tears,
The torment of her holding back;
And though we try, still she will cry
But sometimes my pillow is damp.

Paternity

My inheritance from Chance:
One penny
And this hole in the ground.

There is the dark we see
When we peel off our eyes.

We lie about the cold womb,
Wishing on remembered stars
For the Great Perhaps.

Trace the copper Janus head
With a Judas thumb.
There is memory in those lines
Like riverbeds.
Engravings that murmur ribald rhyme,
Abrasive to the nerve until it
Is worn away.

I remember that I don't remember
But I remember that I used to know.
Perhaps Chance is not our father
Perhaps we are not the sun but the moon.

Lost in the Dark

Part I. Not Guilty

Ring around the rosy,
Pockets full of poesy,
Ashes, ashes,
We all fall down.

There was a stallion in the distance,
Whickering the wind
That tumbled
Over the four-post Evergreen fence.

The stallion came
With the setting sun,
A mounted knight who recited eulogies
In a strangled voice.

He said he was once a wooden boy
Who found a sleeping child
After slaying a dragon
And finding the owner of a glass slipper.

When I penetrated his bony flesh
I felt his inner art:
Unfinished sculptures, paintings,
And classic rhymes;
Unfinished but sincere.

I saw the glass slipper under his bed.
He said it was left by a burglar
Once upon a time.

Part II. Prince Charming

Once upon a time
He swept me off my feet
Away from white pickets and low tides
With tidy sand scraped in a fist.
He whispered sweet fidelity and
Clumsy rhyme
From sandpaper lips

And we lived happily ever after.
There is a worn rock I fall under.
The pursuing horse
Breathes the sand into fist-sized circles
All around my rock,
The sun eclipsed by my errant
Mounted knight.
I weep sandy tears when the wind blows and
Hides the dusty knight that demands a dance.

He is a proud stallion.
Weeping while laughing,
Laughing while weeping,
Laughing and swallowing all that I am;
Because we are destined to heal the sick and raise
The dead.

He only comes when I can't spin straw into gold.
He only comes when I don't say his name.

His closet smells like corpses
Hiding glittered, gallows glass;
Glass shoes for a noose
And glass splinters urge him to not hold back.

Part III. Black Hat Snow White

The only way out is through.

Fairies lie romantic sighs
Waiting for knights to bring rings and roses;
Gold and red hide black and blue.

Maidens cry with lustful eyes,
Abandon knights in confusing fog
For princes who lie about being frogs.

Love spent in flesh looks for more
And trades Cinderella's dress
For a hat, cauldron and tongue of dog.

Blacken eyes with the truest lies that bleed
Riverbeds worn in sorrowed flesh
And scar and sour.

The salty tears leave only salt
Beneath the breaking sigh

That roots in our graves:

Buck your rider,
Bury him deep.
Break the slipper over his back
Bear glass splinters in our eyes
That bleed us dry.

Part IV. Black Hole Manifesto

Ashes serve as tourniquets
For limping cadavers
Preserved in life's holocaust:
The amnesiac dead.
Skeletons stumble in staccato step
Spit from stain-glass closets,
Slithering with hollow lollypops
That sucker children to cemeteries.

Every step sings muted death
In maraca rhythm, a monocidal plod,
That paints the sky a vivid lie
To pretend there is no sun.

The bells that toll, that toll for us,
Accuse with apocalyptic trust,
Reap us to the guy on the cross
We limp and drone,
Lost
Lost

Lost

Let us proclaim the mystery of faith:

We are
The silence after
The scream on the wind.

The Gravedigger

Sepulcher silence
Where wooden boys raged
And whores have tried;
Sandpaper knights with wooden sighs
Have believed mirrored lies
Spit by a princess with frog's eyes.

Death-begotten dead, torpor-content
Sharing the holocaust of meaning;
Life entombed in love's memory.
Such is the intimacy of corpses:
Many longings in one grave.

Dreamless we cling together
Unless the specters reappear
To taunt with testimony:
Broken promise,
Bitter words,
You should never have tried.

Adrift in a cadaver raft,
Wedding band epitaphs
Swear truth forever,
Alone.

One breath in death,
An autumn breeze
Stirs corpse-like leaves
In Heaven's anonymous name

And draws sandpaper eyes
To a hand – mistaken for a hand
For the first time.

The memory of hands is the last rattle
Punctuated an epitaph
In shovel-born Earth:

Wedding bands, break.
All longing, takes.
Parents tell your children, never.

Yet hands know only to grasp.
His hands found mine
In time to empty a grave
A CPR gasp to save
This corpse from all longing-traps.

Hands know only to grasp
Only the Hand that fits,
And one size fits all
If nail-pierced at the wrist.

Those hands know how to lift;
Rescue a corpse from its corpse-limits,
Explain why sandpaper knights
Put maidens to flight
When seeding fields with broken glass:
Glass is too heavy.
And hope never lasts

Unless the knight's hand is broken, fast,
Before it hangs death on all trees
Since none can bear the weight he breeds
Alone and in the dark.

Those hands know how to grasp
A cross, a corpse;
Wounded drawn to wounded side
To marvel at resurrection art
That leads any who will grasp it
Out of the dark.

Rain

The rain falls when I am alone;
Deserted in extravagance
And wealthy in estrangement.

Harvested hopelessness
Irrigates familiar contours
Weathered through tense seasons
And empty sunrises.

Silent rivers testify
Ruin, despair and shame
That all the world might stand amazed
But the rain falls when I am alone.

Mortified tributaries
Exhume conceit from a shallow grave

Dislocate self from calcified self
Abandoned to the son's light.

Raindrops feed the grass of Nod
With damp dove eggs
To hatch hope in hope's wasteland;
Fellowship for a friendless Cain.

In the watered memory of loneliness
Corpulent grace consummates
And creates an auto-cannibal
To taste the salted sacrament.

Sorrow shrouded fellowship
Estranges loneliness
For divine extravagance:
The rain falls,
But I am never alone.

Fearfluenza

Shame at her need
Buries screams alive.
He neglects the need
To pretend stability.

Their daughter hears tears
Interred through neglect
That plants doubts in dreams
Of princes who storm towers.

No one is listening, none to call;
Left to escape with pharmaceutical
Hope that plants uncoiling need
In headstone blossoms.

Pallid life drinks blue and red
Leaving dread handcuffed
To police that swallow grief
With manly frowns and meditate
Over Killian's.

Courage taken in white lines
Transmutes terror into talons.
Trying for red in red and blue,
Police meditations make nothing new.

The second dread handcuffed
Instead breeds confidence
That black and blue make all things new;
Leaving blue and red with one more dead.

The telephone howls alone
And evokes a mother's tears;
They testify her falsified
Divinations how her son would die.

Then the media hints some things
Never change. One man jokes
And declaws the foreboding signs
That echo he needs protection
Before someone he loves dies.

His wife counterparts
Shared need with tearful eyes.
Manly frowns façade the doubt
His gun shoots and buries alive.

Shame at her need
Buries screams alive.
He neglects the need
To pretend stability.

Their daughter hears tears
Interred through neglect
That plants doubts in dreams
Of princes who storm towers.

The Memory of Men

Specters on the mountain
Shroud themselves in snow,
Hesitant to haunt
The old valleys.

When spirits yearn for
Birthrights they are rebuked
With ancestral crimes.

When wraiths long to bless
Descendants they are directed
To refrain on pain of exorcism;
Boys conformed to commanded names.

Soon boys exchange toys
For vagabond or violent lives.
No man can be summoned
Beyond the mountain reservation.

Uprooted wild flowers
Scattered on deserted slopes;
A mass grave for men.
New ghosts shelter on the mountain.

A sensible sentence to sustain:
Exile for the wild,
Everyone else is safe.

Lazarus –

Come out.

In Ashes Born

You hid when the fires raged,
When all your days
Were filled with the wage
Of someone else's fear.

You sacrificed to stay alive
All you loved, and read, and cried
To retreat into your bunker
Where memories serve as brothers.

Fearful fires razed
All of you left behind
Abandoned, withdrawn into your mind
Under siege from others' tears.

Then the winds blew
And the ashes stirred in squalls
To sting and cut your cheeks
And eulogize all you had lost.
The wasteland of your treasures
Lies fallow and abused
By the heavy tread of insecure men
Who demand your doubt.

Now whispers stir squalls
And blow embers into infernos,
Leaving only memories
And the memory of fear.

You quarried through the buttressed pillbox
And crawled through filth and shame
To reclaim, from the ashes, your name
And to live for more than memory.

And though the bunker calls you back
Where ashes and tempest had buried
You alive,

Never forget that the fires have cooled
The war is over
And you are still alive.

You are stronger
You are wiser
And never a prisoner
Of all the tears you cried.

Baptized in fire
Christened with cinders
The one who is
In ashes born.

Lover

His love falls like gentle spring rain
Tapping gentleman requests
Every morning.

Raindrops reach out with sunrises
Persuading fresh adventures
Every morning.

Selfish flesh forbids with jealous
Complaints, resentful to wake
Every morning.

But the cool promise of crisp rain
Pleads bold justice, inviting
Every morning.

Weather spills a story urging
Slaying dragons, center stage
Every morning.

Invitations sprinkle new days
Forgetting failure and shame
Every morning.

He yearns for you to share with him
Inspired purpose, glory,
Exalted life.

Tomorrow, do not refuse his
Invitation or stifle
His vast spirit.

Kindness is his bouquet
And virtue his foreplay.

Alive

My life is a post in a wrought iron fence;
Twisted and black,
Recycled back
For supportive use from forsaken mess.
It is heavy, strong, and bears up long
To support and protect anyone met
In worth's worthlessness.

Life is the color that covers the days

When we ask why,
When walls are grey.

It is the breeze over broken glass;
Touring the trash,
Singing praise.

Life is a crowbar that pries open attics,
Desert darkness
For son-lit breath.
Life is a love that brings dance to the dead,
Starvation to bread,
Meaning to needing
Unfilled.

This is our hope when change will not come;
Trusting and strong,
Enduring long
When souls anguish dreams and works left undone
Until we become more than we are
By prizing life and not ceasing to run
From the heart
Till the heart is done.

This is the race run with full intent:
Every breath breathed,
Every dream dreamed
Collapsing into God's arms at the end
Spent and broken,
Wearied token
Of life full-lived, over-loved, truly freed

From guilt and shame.
That I should hear, at the end, my name
Spoken with pride,
Roared from the heights:
Here is one who stands unbound
And did not hold tight till now,
Refused to let the world define
Who he is, or was, and why.

I am his, and he is mine.
That is all I know on Earth
And all I need to know.

CPSIA information can be obtained at www.ICGtesting.com
Printed in the USA
BVOW03s1635060916

460830BV00003B/13/P

9 781634 916004